Release the the Fireflies

Karen Richards

Cover Design: Islam Farid

ISBN: 978-0-6489919-5-3

Foreword

There are very few shared experiences in this
life and grief is one of them. We have all
experienced it in one way or another: the loss of
a spouse, child, parent, grandparent, sibling,
or friend. We have lived grief in all of its forms,
from slow peaceful passing to sudden
traumatic ones. Perhaps grief to you isn't
traditional, per se, in that it finds you in the
form of anticipatory grief, lost love, or
even losing yourself.

In this book of poems and prose, I hope you
will find something to relate to: little pieces
about loved ones I have lost throughout my
life and words that will unlock long-forgotten
memories of your own loved ones in your heart.

You will come to believe that grief is survivable,
and that there is healing to be found even
when it feels impossible.

We are living proof.

CONTENTS

Strands of Sunshine

13   summer boughs
14   smoke
15   shift in the stars
16   hidden tempo
17   upturned
18   coming home
19   infinite wishes
20   blur
21   soul speak
22   moonlit tresses
23   rain on a summer day
24   descending darkness
25   as fall the leaves
26   my smile
27   the impact of goodbye
28   someday
29   little moments
30   a million pieces
31   this breeze
32   memories of you
33   strands of sunshine
34   ancient scars
35   seasons

Descending Darkness

39   lonely places
40   afraid of the dark
41   absent moon
42   when the saddest songs play
43   crying stars
44   forgetting
45   choreographing constellations
46   emptiness
47   favourite t-shirt
48   dawn
49   happiness wilts
50   memory lane
51   promises
52   grief creeps

53   your ashes
54   melancholy blues
55   trembling hands
56   space
57   bruises
58   empty hands
59   bloodied hands
60   grief is just love
61   ache
62   unnatural death
63   hollows of mourning
64   the delicacy of grief

This Moonless Sky

69   when they ask about our undoing
       after @ana.dee.writes
70   epitome of loneliness
71   fields of death
72   hands of time
73   asphyxiating lungs
74   no goodbye
75   things no one told me about grief
       Part I
76   after the fall
77   wistful whispers
78   the sound of tears
79   truth is
80   white pillowcases
81   reckless moon
82   vintage reels
83   flickering
84   band-aids and bullet holes
85   castle
86   imaginarium
87   typewriter keys
88   death on my tongue
89   like a chain
90   cannibal

Crashing Waves

95   fate
96   flowers
97   I miss you
98   hold on

99   things I love instead of you

100   things you are not allowed to look at
*after @e.tstockdale_*

101   into the dawn

102   things now empty without you

103   things I can't text you - *after @paro.__*

104   crimson burning

105   if I knew where it hurt - *after @seekingthepurpose*

106   tell me there is more than this

107   ways to heal my heart

108   like a blade on my skin

109   lies

110   when the moon is the trigger
that takes me back to your death

111   bitter

112   brittle bones

113   darker days

114   landmine

115   blank pages

116   stolen

117   too sharp

118   forsaken

119   outstretched arms

120   deathly slow

121   untether

122   things no one told me about grief II
(12 months on)

123   jagged edges

124   the delicacy of grief

Reclaiming Rainbows

129   moving on

130   the weight of your memory

131   before it started to hurt

132   meadows of misery

133   it hurts

134   carrying you

135   dear grief

136   lucky

137   when you ask me why I write poetry
*after @isabelrocio_*

138   breaking dawn

139   I promise I won't write about you
after @poms.c.h.s

140   rise
141   when I tell you I lost myself in winter
after @nick.olah.poetry
142   heaven on earth
143   my trauma didn't make me strong
after @Nik_poetry
144   healing
145   before you leave
146   to dream
147   rising light
148   lessons
149   broken pieces
150   waiting for you
151   let love shine
152   stifled
153   I'm sorry it took me so long
to respond to this - *after @e.l.withem*
154   dear august

Release the Fireflies

159   if you turned me inside out, you'd find
160   dreams
161   eloquence
162   one more moment
163   gentle vibration
164   lonely valleys
165   I am a loose thread unravelling
166   liquorice skies
167   how to tell me you love me
168   tilting my heart
169   eyes wide open
170   ribboned constellations
171   parched shores
172   the public art of healing
173   I am a wreckage
174   still polaroids
175   hazel eyes
176   dog-eared pages
177   when they ask how it felt, say
178   bare stems
179   a love letter to you
180   light keeper
181   halfway to heaven
182   stilled hourglass

Strands of Sunshine

summer boughs

I always fell gently
a breeze-kissed leaf
trying in vain to cling
to summer boughs
not yet ready to fall
then, along came you

smoke

his words resemble smoke
curling like soft whispers
from beguiling lips,
pressed against delicate
curves of my neck
raising my body heat
by one hundred degrees,
a waft of alliteration
creeping serpent-like
across my skin
inhaled into my lungs
until every ounce of breath
is exhaled

if there is one thing
I know about him
where there is smoke
there is fire

shift in the stars

this shift in the stars
sees hope cascading
through my veins
faithful constellations
at home in my hands
in your eyes
and in your promise
of forever

hidden tempo

these stars perform
an Argentine tango
filled with longing
hidden in tempo
of unresolved feelings
and unrequited love
'neath a rapturous moon
where I am never left
to dance alone

upturned

the corners of my mouth
are lassoed to stars
a waning crescent
upturned, in the hope
of being closer to you

coming home

what if love
was supposed
to break me
the way it did
so that when
you came along
our pieces
just fit

you feel like
coming home

infinite wishes

come, let's stay a while
in dandelion fields
where infinite wishes
lie in wait
for the impossible
to become magical
with you

blur

I blur into
one hundred and one
shades of you
and I wonder
if it's not
such a bad thing
after all

soul speak

if my soul could speak,
the syllables would pull stars
from the sky
you would ignite in the passion
with which they fall,
so softly from my lips
into the curve of your neck
invisible stains,
inking your skin
captivated by the words
my soul speaks

moonlit tresses

I long for nights
you would climb
moonlit tresses
to paint stars
into midnight skies
just to light my way
home, to your arms

rain on a summer day

love creeps into my bones
as rain on a summer day
seeps into my skin
uninvited, welcomed
cleansing heartbreak
from the empty vessel
I have become
awakening my heart
from a drought

descending darkness

if darkness should descend
and moonbeams fail to shine
I will search for you, in shadows
driven only by the incandescent light,
that is, your heart

as fall the leaves

as fall the leaves, so drop the days
horizon bound, folding delicately
into the earth of hidden truths
meandering darkened valleys
longing to discover
those who are forged by moonlight
as fall the leaves, the lonely are found

my smile

true love is as rare
as rainbows are
without storms
and as my smile
will forever be
without yours

the impact of goodbye

would it hurt less
if we loved in reverse,
already knowing
the impact of goodbye
before it arrived,
or would we live life
counting inevitable seconds
until impact,
never allowing ourselves
to feel, to fall,
to lose ourselves
so completely
into the agony we call love

someday

someday
the only distance between us
will be the close weave
of the clothes we shed,
the whimper of desire
you peel from my lips
with every gentle touch,
the warmth of our bodies
pressed together so intimately
we occupy the same breath
the same skin
the same silhouette
I am lying in wait for someday

little moments

you love me most
when I am weak
in little moments
when your lips
rest against
my forehead
hands, gently folding
the broken
pieces of me
into the shape
of your chest
if now, only
in my dreams

a million pieces

somehow
with a heart
in a million pieces,
each one still belongs
to you

this breeze

I want to be yours
sitting on our porch swing
sipping cool ginger ale
as a rustling spring breeze
ruffles your overgrown curls
hearing the sigh of my name
on your lips just once more
but dreams like these
were never meant to be ours
when the only breath
on this breeze holds goodbye

memories of you

memories follow me everywhere I go
tucked into the crevices of his smile
in sweet sounds of her laughter
they fold, softly into my silhouette
caressing all the loneliness in me
but I will never forsake the pain
I am honoured to endure a lifetime
with these memories of you

strands of sunshine

I exist beneath
warm strands
of sunshine
yet all I can do
is long for those
familiar shadows
where it is just you
me and the soft glow
of a full moon
one last time

ancient scars

heaven is a whisper
brushed softly
over ancient scars
by faded memories
of his touch

seasons

of all
the seasons
we could
have picked
for love
we chose
the fall

Descending Darkness

lonely places

I have lived
in some
lonely places
but none
as lonely
as a world
without you

afraid of the dark

when he died
he pulled the moon
from my sky

I've been afraid
of the dark
ever since

absent moon

an absent moon
left in its wake
only fractured stars
devoid of all light
just the way I felt
when you left

when the saddest songs play

when the saddest songs play
I think of you and nights
which wrapped us in moonlight
masquerading as forever
and when the music stopped
I found myself alone
on the dance floor
swaying to the tune of my grief
head buried in the chest
of your memory

crying stars

it is so quiet here
in the depths
of my grief
I can almost
hear the stars
crying your name

forgetting

there are moments
when I close my eyes
that memories of you
are so vivid, so tangible
I forget they are not real
and I am engulfed
by the loneliness
of forever

choreographing constellations

twilight leaves no trace
of you upon my skin
no sun to kiss me
the way you did
just a lonely moon
choreographing constellations
across night skies
eliciting the unwritten poetry
within me

emptiness

I am always surprised
by the enormity of emptiness
one lonely night can hold

favourite t-shirt

your scent lingers
in worn creases and folds
every now and then
I trace my fingers along
seams you once wore
pull you across my body
and just for a moment
I can feel you touch me
in all the ways you used to
soft kisses laced with aftershave
linger softly on my skin
like they did
before grief stole everything
but these memories
and your favourite t-shirt

dawn

I reach for you
as if the dawn
of a new day
can ignore
this empty heart

happiness wilts

the secret to happiness wilts
like petals, laden with early morning dew
tears clinging to the lashes of heavy lids
in empty palms and lonely arms
words are no longer spoken or heard
lyrics caressing the aching hollows
your smile used to fill
all, no longer mine to know

memory lane

it hurts to write about you
when meandering memory lane
feels like carving into my heart
even more reasons to miss you

promises

the final tendrils of sunshine
creep over my body
leaving promises
of tomorrows return
but I can't believe them
how I wish I could
for I still remember you too
promised once, to stay

grief creeps

there are days
when grief creeps so quietly
not a single sound
can fill the void
meant to be filled by you

your ashes

what if the only happiness
I will ever know is you
and now without you
all those tender words
infused into love-filled lines
have become dust
committed to the earth
with your ashes

melancholy blues

I am swaddled
by the melancholy blues
of a jealous tide
promises of bridged gaps
between heaven and horizon
yet deserting me with nothing
but the bitter taste of salt
on my lips

trembling hands

the tighter you hold me
the more my body
must keep at bay
this rising guilt
my trembling hands
his memory
and I suffocate
beneath the weight
of all the things
I cannot say

space

I have always believed
it was an emptiness
you left behind
when it has
only ever been space
yearning to be filled
with love

bruises

saying your name
is like pushing
on the bruises
of my heart

it still hurts
just the same

empty hands

all that is left
are these empty hands
and a broken heart
which aches

and memories of
the ones I love
I can't bear
to erase

bloodied hands

bloodied hands fall
needle and thread, clasped
in crimson, trembling distain
reflection, now silenced and true
a marionette without strings
a poet without words
an absence that has become
little more than
a barely beating heart
struggling to survive

grief is just love

they tell me
grief is just love
with no place to go
this pain just proves
I love him more
than anyone
could ever know

ache

I stand, frozen
while the
world turns
I wish
it would ache
the way I do

unnatural death

I long to outgrow this grief
but it would require
an unnatural death
of the moon, stars
and everything else
which reminds me of you

hollows of mourning

I am trapped
in hollows of mourning
my ashen skin
enveloped by the
shadowed crevices
sunshine never finds
and I will remain here
the rest of my days
until memories of you fade
or I do

the delicacy of grief

then come the days
when life is so fragile
the wisp of a memory
can tear open
all we have endeavored to heal

such is the delicacy of grief

This Moonless Sky

when they ask about our undoing

after @ana.dee.writes

there will be silence
no more cries
no more sirens
no more prayers to God to save us
we had barely just begun
or maybe we just lived a lifetime of love
in our fleeting forever

there will be moments
where I wonder if you ever existed at all

and an emptiness, oh an emptiness
which will drag me
with the force of a thousand tides
into a lonely tumultuous sea

we are in the eye of the storm
all is silent, all is still
and this quiet, this quiet
is my unravelling

epitome of loneliness

she walks without
casting a shadow
an epitome
of loneliness
is she

fields of death

in a world engulfed by chaos
you were the only thing
which made sense
a yellow rose thriving
beneath the softest rays of the sun
in undulating fields of death
filling voids in me
only the darkness knew existed
still, nothing could prepare me
for the crushing weight
of petals as they fall

hands of time

I have tried to wind back
the hands of time
to get back to the moment
I last saw your smile
but my hands
are bound by guilt
my cheek, at one
with the concrete
where you last
lay your head
guilt pulsing
through me
in weeping waves

why was I not
strong enough
to save you?

asphyxiating lungs

it is as if the mother of all creation
had exhaled a final breath
from asphyxiating lungs
lips frozen by the uncomfortable silence
of muted words
no chance for goodbye
or hope of wonder to be found
just a descending darkness
which swallowed us both

no goodbye

his eyes always
promised forever
until he left me
with no goodbye

Things no one told me about grief
PART I

Everything goes dark, like trying to find
strands of hope in a moonless sky, I will
see glimpses of you everywhere, most of all
in the eyes of your children who at every
turn remind me you are never truly gone.

It is possible to laugh and cry in the space
of one breath, heartbreak and happiness in
equal measure. Grief comes in waves, it
depends on the day whether it is a ripple or
a tsunami, that I will find my comfort not in
people but in things, like sleeping in your
favourite hoodie because it still smells like
you.

And some days I hate you for leaving me,
then I hate myself because I do, then there
will be those seconds, right before I open
my eyes, when I forget that you are gone,
they will forever be what I live for.

after the fall

there is something to be said
for the way loneliness
catches in your chest
impaled between ribs
a dagger of emptiness

truth is, there is never
a more crushing silence
than that which comes
after the fall

wistful whispers

you come to me
in wistful whispers
gleaming smile
a lonely apparition
in mournful moments
where the asphalt
of roads, unfamiliar
incinerate my soul

without you
I am lost

the sound of tears

this world is so quiet
without you in it
even the sound of tears
hitting my pillow
is more than I can stand

truth is

I didn't think
it was possible
to run out of ways
to tell you I miss you
but the truth is, I have
without words
I am silent
without you
I am empty
without both
I am hollow

white pillowcases

today, mascara
and white pillowcases
were my only defence
against heartbreak
and this river of tears

reckless moon

I sit beneath
a reckless moon
thread my pain
into the arms
of dying constellations

whatever it takes
to hold on

vintage reels

vintage reels project
snippets of your life
onto closed lids
but I can't fathom
why the story unfolds
out of order, a headstone
depicting your demise
before you ever truly
learned to live

flickering

I have always believed
these stars were ever-present
like tiny heartbeats
flickering life into night skies
so, why did they go dark
when yours stopped

band-aids and bullet holes

maybe someday
I will learn
trying to ignore
the pain of losing you
is akin to
placing a band-aid
on a bullet hole

castle

I promised myself
I wouldn't look back
when I left our two-story castle
with the blue door
leading to everything
you held dear
at our garden fully laden
with fragrant yellow roses
and frangipani in bloom
or at my homeless heart
without the one
who made our castle
home

imaginarium

if I spend the rest
of my life
writing about you
it is only because
these words
are a life vest
keeping me
from drowning
in the imaginarium
of memories
I wish I was still
making with you

typewriter keys

the truth is
every page to follow
will be blank
as ink dries
and dust gathers
on idle typewriter keys
we will soon be
just a memory
of lost love

death on my tongue

your name
will continue to dance
like death on my tongue
until I learn
to speak of you
one day
as a memory

like a chain

this grief
like a chain
around my neck
may yet
come in handy
as a weight
to drown these
flashbacks
of the death
of us

cannibal

don't believe those
who tell you
grief is a beautiful thing

grief is nothing more
than a cannibal

Crashing Waves

fate

fate clipped our wings
and while you
soared to heaven
I plummeted to earth
shattered beyond repair

flowers

why did you bring me flowers
so, I could witness your death repeating
as every withering petal fell
and thorny stems reminded me
just how much losing you hurt

I miss you

I miss you. so much, emptiness wails through
the white walls of our room. I miss the way
you reached for me before opening your eyes,
a familiar comfort, now glaringly hollow against
cold sheets of an empty bed. I see now, how
little pieces of me crept into your life,
unwillingly, unknowingly before we finally
understood love, a single piece of paper taped
to a mirror, the first poem I ever wrote for you,
with all its little mistakes scribbled out. I guess
things make sense now, we made plenty on
our road together.

I miss the feeling of your lips against my
forehead when I am sad and baby I am so
sad without you. The way you held me so tightly
I didn't know where you ended and I began.
I miss our nights cozied up by the fire, talking
about everything and nothing long into the
night because you knew I was in love with the
moon but never as much as I was with you.
Perhaps this will get easier, stop hurting so
much, then again maybe I don't want it to
because while it hurts this much

I can still feel enough, to miss you

hold on

they keep telling me to hold on
that tomorrow will be better
when all I want is to go back
to that night and beg you
to take me too

things I love instead of you

the silent quell and quiet between
bone-crushing waves drowning demons in
my head before they devour my sanity and
remnants of you

the rain, because how else am I supposed
to camouflage the deluge pouring from
eyes to cheeks to overflowing palms

the lies I tell myself, to make it okay,
to make it hurt less, to make myself believe
that somewhere out there, you still love
me too

things you are not allowed to look at
*after @e.tstockdale_*

these trembling hands
the play count of our favourite song
my quivering lip when they talk about you
the pile of mascara-stained pillowcases
my growing collection of scars
the remnants of love in the urn
beside my bed

my shattered heart

into the dawn

I long to tuck myself
into the dawn
to languish in light
my soul, painted
in hues of hope
before the gloom
manifests itself
beneath my skin
coaxing demons
from my pores
just to drag me
into the darkness
once again

things now empty without you

the old worn-out recliner which somehow
survived the weight of our love, all the tears
which fell against your chest as it burst at the
seams, trying to squeeze two into a space
meant for one

the lyrics to every song we ever danced to,
cheek to cheek under the moonlight, melted
in your arms beneath stars which twinkled
in my eyes for only you, and in every song,
we will never get to dance to again

your side of the bed, where there is no one
to hold me the way you did. no promises
that everything will be ok this time, where
time heals nothing and there is no moving
on, no letting go, just a broken heart,
learning to love a ghost

things I can't text you
after @paro.___

I am suffocating on all the words tightly
coiled around my throat, the blame crushing
the air from my lungs until I am left
clutching my chest, begging for mercy

I want to press pause on this moment
before I completely forget the little things
before you are simply a silhouette in my
dreams and your smile becomes something
I used to know

I am not strong enough to hold the weight
of your world, to be everything they need.
You should have believed me when I told
you I was nothing

the moon can't heal me anymore, it doesn't
understand my pain the way it did, choosing
to hide behind clouds so it can't witness
my tears, now I have nowhere to call home

I deleted your number today, they say it's
time, time to move on, move forward,
just move. I'm not ready, I'll never be ready,
to let you go

crimson burning

tides of watered-down words
press themselves to my tongue
dance on crimson burning
of bruised, bitten lips
in desperate attempts
to hold back these floodgates of pain

if I knew where it hurt
after @seekingthepurpose

maybe I could find peace, I could stop using
shiny blades to search my own pale flesh for
a cause. I wouldn't need to sit in the dark,
night after night doing math in my head,
just how many pills will it take to make it
stop.

if I knew where it hurt, I could plug every
hole with the love I am cradled with and stop
myself from bleeding out, but grief is not a
wound to be healed, a cancer to be cured,
a broken bone to be set, grief is a lesson in
endurance, kindness, forgiveness, acceptance.

believe me, I know every inch of where it
hurts but it is a sentence from which, I never
wish to be saved

tell me there is more than this

more than this concrete jungle of sadness filled
with sunshine that holds no warmth, blooms of
pink frangipani without fragrance, and silently
raging seas

tell me there is more than this emptiness, this
cavern of hollowness, this inability to form a
single word with a mouth that just longs to
kiss you again

more than finding you, everywhere in everything
I look at or touch, in songs I hear but never how
I need you most, here

tell me there is more than grief which follows
me like a black dog, begging for a home with
pleading eyes I can't deny for fear it will be
lost and so will you

ways to heal my heart

remove the noose from my neck, use it
instead to hang the demons who want to take
my life, pull it tight and let me hear them beg
for forgiveness as they die, just make sure they
don't kill me first

love me, when it is too hard, when I am not
worthy, when I don't know how to love you
back, to love myself, to tell you where it hurts,
why it hurts, how much it hurts

hold me like you mean it, like you used to, like
you promised you would even if you don't
mean it anymore

like a blade on my skin

this darkness
weighs heavily
like a blade
on my skin

please
let me drown
in the flood

lies

I'm tired of living a life
where every breath
is a lie I tell
to convince you
I'm strong enough
to go on

**when the moon is the trigger that takes
me back to your death**

I can no longer face the dark, where once it
was a place of solace, I now find only tears and
memories. I find myself winding back time, day
after day *(I want to make this end differently)* perhaps
the sound of breaking as I tried to save you, was
not your chest but my heart *(some things when broken,
can never be healed)* I dream of laying my head on
your heart just to hear it beat again *(please god
just let it beat again)* maybe I'm not afraid of the
dark at all *(maybe I'm just afraid of being lost in the
darkness with the void meant for you)*

bitter

why do words
never taste as sweet
as they sound
once, love, and forever
tasted like honey
now they roll
from my tongue
bitter, like grief

brittle bones

there is nothing I can do
to make you stay
no way to help you find worth
when unworthiness
has lived a lifetime
deep-seated in
these brittle bones

please don't ask me
why my hands are so cold
my arms, so frail
they are unable
to hold onto love
tell me instead
why do they always leave

darker days

they beg me to brush away
the darker days
to be stronger than that
which pulls me towards him
into the chasmal void
we call death

landmine

this poem
is a landmine
by which I mean
with these words
I blew it all away

blank pages

I toss words
at blank pages
trying desperately
to make this pain
seep into anything
but my heart

I am tattooed, eternally
with memories of you

stolen

goodbye has stolen
the moon and stars
I am lost in the dark
without you

too sharp

they are happy
to tear flesh
from your bones
only to turn around
and tell you
those same bones
are too sharp
to be held

forsaken

I hear church bells ringing
and I contemplate praying
but for what reason
he proved me forsaken
the moment he stole
your heartbeat away

outstretched arms

I search for you in sunsets, with outstretched
arms and palms upturned, trying in vain to
cup a dying amber sun between them, to
stop it fleeing, before this night blindness
sets in and I can no longer find you in the
dark.

I find myself howling at the moon, a lost
soul begging for death or at least something
to create a home inside me that doesn't hurt.

I am crucified by the tiny filaments of hope
which try to reach for me, to hold me tight,
while I plead with their maker, please, don't
save me now

deathly slow

it is deathly slow
the way in which
we become accustomed
to inhaling and exhaling
breaths we wish
were never born

untether

I tear moonbeams
from my chest
untethering you
from these burdens
please, don't waste time
clinging, hopefully
to what is already gone

Things no one told me about grief –
PART II
(12 months on)

There is no solace in empty arms, in gardens
of wilted hydrangeas of seasons passed. I will
lose the ability to smile with reckless abandon
or press my face towards the sun without
thoughts of you. Muscle memory will still exist
in those snippets of time when I reach for you
across an empty bed and find only loneliness.
That people won't love you the same way, they
will love you, yes, but from a distance and with
silent tongues. Tsunamis are survivable, even
when you want them to swallow you whole.
Whole will become a term you learn to use
only in past tense, when speaking of the former
you, the BHD (before he died) you. That grief
left shattered pieces of you strewn across the
rest of your life and expects you to piece back
together what can only be done by the person
it took and looking back now, grief has taught
me that love is infinite, irreplaceable,
immeasurable and it teaches me with every
new day, a new and more heartbreaking way,
to miss you

jagged edges

she folded herself like origami
into shapes of nothingness
and for the first time
she found peace
in jagged edges
now sharp enough
to take her life

the delicacy of grief

such is the delicacy of grief
it can make
grenades from gerberas
machetes from memories
poison from poetry
and leaves me wondering
if there has ever been
a more painful warfare
than this

Reclaiming Rainbows

moving on

I know life has moved on
when they ask me
to miss you
just a little more quietly

the weight of your memory

I am not yet ready
to embrace the reality
that this empty heart
will bury me, still breathing
beneath the weight
of your memory

before it started to hurt

we were butterfly tattoos, inked into each
other's flesh, rule breakers who stole the
best pieces of each other with wild abandon,
early morning texts, and late- night
rendezvous, everything we promised we
would never be, we were amber lights never
approached with caution, summer sunsets
and raging winter flames, hardened hearts
learning what it meant to love and be loved
and always a soft place to fall, imperfectly
perfect just as true love should be before
fate took your hand and demolished it all

meadows of misery

I keep planting hope
in meadows of misery
fold memories of you
into furling petals
for safekeeping
sheltered from the amnesia
of this hopeless heart

it hurts

it hurts

loving you

missing you

still, I dread the day

when it won't

carrying you

if I look back now
I can see
the moment
our footprints
in the sand
became one
now I must learn
to walk alone

carrying you
only
in my heart

dear grief,

I think you believe we are friends, a
bonded pair with no beginning or end,
like shadows cast against light. Perhaps
it is true, I have come to depend on you,
as clockwork as day and night, rain and shine,
an embrace I long for because it is my love
for him you hold tenderly in your hands,
our memories you offer up to my broken
heart and maybe, just maybe because
whenever you are near, he is too.

lucky

I spent my life
never understanding
the beauty of love
how one could give
all of themselves to another
yet remain whole

it has taken you leaving
for me to truly comprehend
how lucky I was to love
and be loved with more light
than a universe of stars
a light, I must harness
to fill all the empty space
you left behind

when you ask me why I write poetry
after @isabelrocio_

when you ask why I write poetry
I tell you it is like an olive branch
offered by my closed mind
to my open heart, apologising
for the pain it has caused

breaking dawn

I search for you in breaking dawns
in a vast emptiness of ocean
draping itself on desolate shores
I yearn for a touch of comfort
or familiarity with your smile
even if home is now
far beyond blazing burnt horizons
far beyond the endless emptiness I feel
I will forever be drawn home
to the dawning of the sea
where I am promised your smile
in still reflections of me

I promise I won't write about you
after @poms.c.h.s

so instead, I will sprawl in green grass,
twirling lavender sprigs between wistful
fingers while I search clouds for the shape
of your face.

Alexa will ask what I want to hear and I
will reply 'anything that reminds me of him'
she already knows how this story ends.

I will search the mirror for any trace of the
girl you fell in love with but find nothing
left to love, then I will concede defeat and
pick up my pen before I drown in the
syllables of your name

rise

I have been wearing
the ocean every day
since you left
clinging to waves
for dear life
frantically treading water
beneath the surface
it has just taken me
too long to realise
it was never your intention
to let me drown
but to watch me rise
and learn to swim
on my own

when I tell you I lost myself in winter
after @nick.olah.poetry

it is true, I stripped bare, my soul and buried
it beneath freshly fallen snow. witnessed
heavy boots of loneliness carelessly trample
my weary bones. carved fragile ribs into
pointed spears aimed directly at my heart.

I'll be honest, I prayed for death or at least
solace from the voices in my head, instead,
the unwelcome infiltration of pain arrived
with the sole intent to plant death in every
crevice of my soul but it underestimated me,
all it served was a reminder of my strength,
will and bravery

every season has a purpose and winter taught
me, mine was to rise

heaven on earth

I've since realised home
is now in those
who have your eyes
wear your smile
love me with open arms
and share my love for you

home is the heaven on earth
you entrusted me with
when you left

my trauma didn't make me strong

after @nik_poetry

but it proved that I can be engulfed by flood,
with hands still steady enough to shoulder
the weight of an umbrella, protecting hearts
from the corrosive rains of grief and I am
capable of creating rainbows from the
aftermath of any storm, by using every lost
piece of me to build it

no, my trauma didn't make me strong

it has shown me I always was

healing

one of the
hardest parts
of losing you
is knowing
each step I take
towards healing
is another step
away from you

before you leave

tell me I am more than syllables in goodbye,
more than the pull of bright lights and fresh
pages of new books, more than copious
shared sunsets beneath different skies and
tides which turned our hearts inside out

see me for who I am, not who I was when
we met, see me broken if you must but know
these pieces of me would have blown away
long before now, without you, see the tears
I hide when I am scared, alone, standing on
a pier, waving farewell, so long, until we meet
again

hold me, not the way lovers do but, in your
heart, where it matters, where I matter, let
your heart fill with the pride I feel, watching
you stand in a spotlight you were born for,
watching your smile return home

know you are loved beyond measure, beyond
words, beyond all else, always, and evermore

to dream

I was always afraid of the dark
scared to close my eyes to dream
now asleep is all I want to be
in hope that you are there
waiting for me

rising light

as poetry fell
filling these dark
empty spaces
I caught sight
of the rising light
held down
by the fear
of my grief

lessons

all this time
I believed it was you
who made me strong
when in fact
you were teaching me
ways to find strength
in myself

broken pieces

no one can hold
your broken pieces
as gently as hands
wanting to heal them

waiting for you

as daylight nestles snuggly
into cradles of night
I tiptoe through infinite darkness
swaddle myself in a cocoon of stars
and the soft caress of a lonely moon
waiting for you to find me
where you always find me
a speck of light in the darkness
of my grief

let love shine

I had tied constellations
in knots so tightly
around my heart
to protect what once was
I had forgotten
how good it feels
to let our love shine
even if just for the
angels to see

stifled

I am stifled by the burden
of who I was
the grief of those
I have lost
and longing for who
I might become
if I could just learn
to breathe

I'm sorry it took me so long to respond to this
after @e.l.withem

I've been lost, so lost I couldn't find the
strength to tell you where to find me, a
compass pointing its arrow to my heart like
I didn't know where it hurt like I hadn't
noticed my toes dangling over the edge in
a teeter on the cusp of insanity

I've been lost, alone in the wilderness,
sheltering myself beneath safe boughs of
self-preservation, languishing in piles of
autumn leaves, afraid of being lost, afraid of
being found, just afraid

I've been busy finding myself, building
bridges between my heart and mind, letting
time heal wounds I thought would never
mend, learning to love the scars they left
behind, accepting that I am as broken as I
am whole, I'm sorry it took me so long to
respond to this, I've been busy finding the
love I lost, in myself

dear august,

I'd like to say you left me in a better state
than you found me but faded black and blues
tell the truth, you held my face against freshly
painted walls while you took from me, any
ounce of sanity I had left, wrapped hands around
my throat as I lay, sprawled on bloody sheets
and told me, I would never amount to more
than this moment, this season. I almost believed
you, let your wintery chill blanket my bones,
allowed it to bury me beneath the purity of a
final winter snow where no one would ever
find me but you forgot one thing, spring is
my season, my siren song, the efflorescent
calling to which I cling in anticipation of
happiness, my kaleidoscopic splendor.

you took my life in august, but I will return,
september's child, ready to bloom anew.

Release the Fireflies

if you turned me inside out, you'll find

the roar of a wild ocean, pulsing through
my veins

the soft pink pigment of a thousand sunsets

every held breath for promises made but
never delivered

the lyrics of every song we danced to,
trapped beneath my tongue

the cool breeze that shook my bones and
found me a home in your arms

memories of everything that has broken me
and all that has made me whole

dreams

as daylight softly swoops
into the arms of night
so too am I
consumed by dreams
of a world
where again
you are mine

eloquence

there is no eloquent way
to say this
but I miss
being loved by you

one more moment

if I could have just
one more moment
it would be slow dancing
beneath mirror ball stars
feeling your heart beating
rhythmically against me
where no song felt
as empty as they do now
so I could kiss you
softly, one more time
and tell you
I found my forever
in you

gentle vibration

to help her
I need to place my faith
in the gentle vibration
of all the love
that still beats within me
still longing for a place
to call home

lonely valleys

I am always facing west
perhaps that's why I never
see the sun rise
or capture the dawn of a new day
why I am trapped in material memories
of you, of us
of everything the sun set upon
why I am trapped behind darkened hills
and in the depth of lonely valleys
where colours are as dull
as the ache in my heart

maybe it's time to face east
to feel the warmth of love
kiss my cold skin
let it fill my empty palms
with more, more than this
monochromatic existence
this melancholic misery
of life without you

I am a loose thread unravelling

I am a loose thread unravelling from the
collar of his favourite blue knitted sweater,
a keepsake that once held me feather-like
against his chest, proving a soft place to fall
did exist in his arms. Now spring is here,
the sweater is threadbare, and my hands
are full, it has become less about him and
more about me using these threads of us,
to knit something that will keep me warm
at night, that fits the person who is trying
to grow, outside the blues of his favourite
knitted sweater.

liquorice skies

amid a sour taste of liquorice skies
you found me, folding my pain
into damp, tear-stained napkins
which tore beneath their weight
I searched your eyes for goodbye
but never found anything less
than eager arms holding me
safely against heartbeats of hope
salvation that saw me outlive
gloomy nights I never imagined I could
held together by little moments of hope
and you

how to show me you love me

show me fields of dandelions, tell me every
detail of their beauty, press your wishes to
the wind which carries them, prove you
believe there is more to magic than meets
the eye

see past my scars, prove to me, that they
change nothing even when they change
everything, show me how you have been
broken and survived

sit across from me while we eat your
favourite meal, and talk, I don't mean
about nothing, tell me something no one
knows, let my existence mean something
to you

don't look at me that way with pitying eyes,
see me as feeble or weak when you don't
know the strength I have harnessed to get
me this far

show up every day, even when I am too
much or not enough, whether I tell you
I need you and even when I can't

STAY

tilting my heart

I survived last year
holding your memory
like crumpled autumn leaves
I refused to let fall
but our season has passed
a new year has begun
soon flowers will blossom
promising all that is new
and I, my love
must tilt my heart
toward the sun's warmth
if I am ever to learn
how to thrive in this life
alone

eyes wide open

such is the longing
to close my eyes
to sleep, to dream
to find you where
you wait for me
but the time has come
for healing, for hope
and to dream
with eyes wide open

ribboned constellations

today I unraveled
these ribboned
constellations of you
from my skin
who knew
without you
I could be whole

parched shores

darling, you are more
more than the sum
of all this pain
you are cool water
gifted to parched shores

if only you would believe

the public art of healing

only through the public art
of healing
will those facing
deserted cobblestones of grief
learn, there is more to life
than this

I am a wreckage

I am a wreckage
brimming with debris
handfuls of stardust
born of my own demise
moon rubble
swallowed eagerly
by threadbare hearts
with wanton eyes
drowning in
purged paragraphs
of a tired tongue
somehow, still
intrinsically laced
with hope

still polaroids

darkness cannot distort
memories of your love
nor steal from me
still polaroids of you
kept safely in my mind
if tonight I choose to dream
of the magic we were

hazel eyes

we crossed paths today
she is nothing like I remember
coy smile hiding a story
her hazel eyes can't
but she is happy
she is happy
and she is whole

dog-eared pages

I will dog-ear the pages of our story
and return to them
whenever my heart
needs a miracle to hold onto

when they ask how it felt, say

it felt like two people learning to waltz
with two left feet

like touching toes to a gentle lap of cool
water after crossing miles of hot sand

tell them it felt like the eye of the storm,
calm and serene, while the world raged
outside

say it felt like one of those dreams,
where you cannot find reality, no matter
how you try

that it felt like a handful of Polaroid
moments, decorating a refrigerator,
memories of long forgotten forevers

say it hurt, the kind of pain you welcome
when you finally find true love

bare stems

like a flower
our love still lives
pruned back to bare stems
beneath tear-laden clouds
but still nurtured
to blossom into something
longer lasting
than life itself

a love letter to you

another season has passed, full of bright
blue skies and a warmth my body so badly
needed. I didn't see you as much as seasons
passed by perhaps it was that I was blinded
by the sunshine of new beginnings, new days,
new hope.

I thought I would miss you less, that these
feelings would somehow subside, and I would
no longer ache, but grief doesn't work that way,
it takes your happiest days and adds a little
streak of black, takes perfection, and fills it
with doubt.

sadly, I'll admit I have forgotten the sound
of your voice and scent of your favourite
cologne but I still can't forget you. I know
you'll have that twinkling smile in your eye
because you see what was born from losing
you, how you changed me in every perfect
way love should change a person.

please don't worry, this is not a goodbye,
it is just that I have a life to live. I'll see you
in the stars and meet you in my dreams,
forever and always

light keeper

only now
storm clouds
billowing
in my wake
do I realise
I was the
light keeper
all along

release
the fireflies

halfway to heaven

meet me halfway to heaven
where the death
of shooting stars
is captivating
and we are as infinite
as the blush of the moon

stilled hourglass

grief is a time traveller
and there will always
be a part of me
bags packed and ready
to return home
moonlight in my eyes
stilled hourglass in hand

ABOUT THE AUTHOR

Karen Richards resides in Australia, and she is a writer of poetry and prose, the author of two poetry collections *Wrapped in Folds of Midnight* and *The Way My Words Fall*.

Karen has been writing poetry for over 30 years and enjoys connecting with her audience with emotion and simplicity through shared experiences. Her poetry has also been featured in many anthologies over the last few years.

Karen currently writes to a social media audience and her work can be found on Instagram.